Read All About Dogs

CANINE COMPANIONS

Barbara J. Patten

The Rourke Corporation, Inc.
Vero Beach, Florida 32964

6867824

PHOTO CREDITS
Photos courtesy of Corel

Library of Congress Cataloging-in-Publication Data

Patten, Barbara J., 1951-
    Canine companions / by Barbara J. Patten.
        p. cm. — (Read all about dogs)
    Includes index.
    Summary: Illustrations and brief text present various breeds of dogs known as companions, or nonsporting dogs, including the Dalmation, keeshond, poodle and Shar-Pei.
    ISBN 0-86593-455-X
    1. Dogs—Juvenile literature.   2. Dog breeds—Juvenile literature.
3. Dogs—Social aspects—Juvenile literature. [1. Dogs.]
I. Title II. Series: Patten, Barbara J., 1951- Read all about dogs.
SF426.5.P37   1996
636.7'2—dc20   96–23069
                                                                    CIP
                                                                    AC

Printed in the USA

TABLE OF CONTENTS

NONSPORTING DOGS

Nonsporting is the name given to the group of dogs that help people feel good by being their friends. Some visit sick children in hospitals or elderly people in nursing homes. A wagging tail can be good medicine.

Canines (KAY nynz), or dogs, in this group are usually small to medium size. They like people, are full of energy, and learn commands easily.

Let's read all about the nonsporting group and meet some new canine friends.

The Boston terrier is a small dog that was first bred in the city of Boston.

LHASA APSOS

Peek under all the hair on a **Lhasa apso** (LAH suh) (AP so) and you will find a sturdy dog with dark eyes, long whiskers, and a tail that curls over its back.

Lhasa apsos have excellent hearing, which they use to guard their homes and families. Of course, good ears are a must with all that hair over the eyes.

The Lhasa apso's coat grows long enough to trail over the floor.

TIBETAN TERRIERS

Summertime in Tibet finds these dogs shaved and their hair woven into cloth.

Larger than the Lhasa apso, but just as hairy, is the Tibetan terrier.

Long ago, in the country of Tibet, selling these dogs was thought to bring bad luck. People gave them as gifts to show thanks or respect.

Sometimes used to herd sheep, most Tibetan terriers are family pets. Their odd bark that sounds like a siren makes them fine watchdogs.

DALMATIANS

The **Dalmatian** (dal MAY shun) is known for its spots. Dalmatian pups, though, are born pure white. Their spots begin to appear when they are about five weeks old.

Years ago, Dalmatians were called "coach dogs" because they would trot beside horse-drawn carriages.

These spotted canines also cleared the way for horse-drawn firetrucks racing to fires. Dalmatians still serve as mascots, or signs of good luck, to firemen everywhere.

The playful, but protective, Dalmatian makes a dependable family dog.

KEESHONDS

A wolfy gray coat and marks around the eyes, like glasses, make the **keeshond** (KAYS HAWNT) a dog of special beauty.

Their thick coats are waterproof, and they're terrific swimmers. Keeshonds once traveled the oceans with Dutch sailors and were handy at catching rats and mice below deck.

Loyal and alert, keeshonds make wonderful family pets.

Keeshonds look like wolves, but their gentle personalities make them popular companions.

BULLDOGS

Its courage, calmness, and tough looks have earned it the honor of mascot for the United States Marine Corps. "It" is the **bulldog** (BOOL dawg).

Over 100 years ago in England, bulldogs weighing almost a hundred pounds were used as fighting dogs.

The bulldog is the mascot for the United States Marine Corps.

The bulldog's muscles make it one of the strongest breeds of its size.

Today, bulldogs weigh about 50 pounds and are raised to be friendly. They get along well with children and make good guard dogs for families.

BICHON FRISÉS

A pleasant bark and bouncing trot are marks of the **bichon frisé** (bee SHAHN) (free ZAY).

Bichon frisés once lived in the palaces of Spain and France. Later they were often seen in circus acts.

Today, the bichon frisé is valued as family pet and pal, though this lively little dog has a mind of its own.

A white double coat gives the bichon frisé its fluffy look.

POODLES

Do you think poodles like their fancy haircuts?

Poodles do like attention from people, even if it means standing still for a clipping.

Shaving a poodle's curly, thick coat was first done to help it swim more easily when getting ducks for hunters.

Poodles come in three sizes and several solid colors. These good-natured pets are known for being smart dogs. They seem to understand words better than any other breed.

Without clipping every 6 to 8 weeks, a poodle's coat becomes a tangled mess.

SHAR-PEIS

The **Shar-Pei** (SHAHR PAY) looks like a puppy in grown-up skin. Big wrinkles cover its body.

A long time ago in China, people raised Shar-Peis to fight. Their deep folds of skin gave them some protection.

Today, Shar-Peis are raised to be "buddies." They are loyal, calm dogs that make good playmates for children.

This Shar-Pei's frown may be hiding a smile inside.

CHOW CHOWS

Sea captains used the word chow chow to describe their cargo, which often included these dogs.

Except for a blue-black tongue, the **chow chow** (CHOW chow) is a teddy bear look-alike.

Hundreds of years ago in China these dogs were raised for pulling carts and sleds.

Chow chows look out for themselves and are known for patience with their masters.

YOUR COMPANION DOG

After reading about nonsporting dogs, you may start to think about a canine companion of your own.

One of these dogs could bring loads of fun into your life—like having a best friend who never has to go home.

All dogs need clean water, wholesome food, medical care, and a warm, safe place to live. Just like people, they need love and attention, too.

Owning a dog is a big job. You are responsible for the life of your canine companion.

The Dalmatian is known for its spots.

GLOSSARY

bichon frisé (bee SHAHN) (free ZAY) — a small, sturdy dog, with a wavy white coat, drooping ears, and an upwardly curved tail

bulldog (BOOL DAWG) — a short-haired dog with large head; strong, square jaws; and stocky body

canine (KAY nyn) — of or about dogs; like a dog

chow chow (CHOW chow) — heavy-set dog with a long red or black coat and blue-black tongue; also called "chow"

Dalmatian (dal MAY shun) — a dog with a short, smooth white coat covered with black or dark brown spots; also called "carriage dog" and "coach dog"

keeshond (KAYS HAWNT) — a breed from the Netherlands that has a thick gray-blue coat

Lhasa apso (LAH suh) (AP so) — a small dog from Tibet having a long, straight coat

Shar-Pei (SHAHR PAY) — a breed from China having large muscles, wrinkled skin, and a smooth coat

Dogs depend on their human friends to keep them safe and healthy.

INDEX